Little David Learns to Earn a Lot of Money

The Blessed Creation

Published by The Blessed Creation, 2023.

LITTLE DAVID LEARNS TO EARN A LOT OF MONEY

First edition. April 5, 2023.

Copyright © 2023 The Blessed Creation.

ISBN: 979-8215164365

Written by The Blessed Creation.

Also by The Blessed Creation

How to Pray a Good Prayer and Simple Guide for Normal People and
Get Answered (With Testimonies)
Panda Panda Bear What Do You Learn: With Jokes and Quizzes
Little David Learns to Earn a Lot of Money

Table of Contents

We would like to say BIG thanks to ALL person who deeply involved to make this inspirational book published! Great book for kids and everyone.

Little David Learns to Earn a Lot of Money

PREFACE

HOLD ONTO YOUR HATS, because Little David's story is a wild ride from start to finish!

Little David is a young boy with a mission - to buy the Latest Version of The Electronic Toys of his dreams. As every kid knows, Electronic Toys don't come cheap, and Little David's pocket money is barely enough to buy a bag of chips. So he decides to take matters into his own hands and start earning some serious cash!

With boundless energy and a never-say-die attitude, Little David embarks on a series of hilarious and sometimes outrageous adventures, from mowing lawns and delivering newspapers, to babysitting and selling lemonade. Along the way, he discovers that making money isn't just about hard work - it's also about creativity, ingenuity, and a healthy dose of risk-taking. With the help of his parents, his family, his friends and his teachers, Little David navigates the ups and downs of entrepreneurship, learning valuable lessons about money management, customer service, and the power of campaign. From the highs of making his first big sale to the lows of losing his earnings. Little David faces every challenge with courage and enthusiasm.

In a small town not too far away, there was a little boy named David who loved nothing more than spending his pocket money on sweets and toys. Every week, he would eagerly wait for his parents to hand over his allowance so he could run to the nearest candy store and indulge in his favorite treats. But one day, something happened that changed Little David's perspective on money forever. He overheard his parents talking about how they struggled to make ends meet and how important it was to save money for the future. Little David was surprised and a little scared by this news, as he had never really thought about money beyond spending it on himself.

Feeling a newfound sense of responsibility and his dream to own the latest version of The Electronic Toys, Little David decided to learn how to earn his own money. He set out on a mission to find ways to increase his pocket money and become more financially independent.

At first, he tried selling some of his old toys and books, but he quickly realized that he needed to think outside the box if he wanted to make a real difference. So he started to learn about the basic money concept, brainstorming new ideas and taking on challenges that would help him earn money, saving, keeping track his money, budgeting and more. He tried his hand at gardening, offering to help his neighbors with their yards in exchange for a small fee. He also started a car-washing service and even began selling his own lemonade with the creative wonderful twist!

But as David started earning more money, he began to face new challenges. He had to learn how to manage his finances, save for the future, and balance his desire for fun with his responsibility to be financially responsible. He also faced many obstacles and had to think creatively to overcome them. He quickly learned that being an entrepreneur wasn't easy, but it was definitely rewarding!

One day, he decided to set up a lemonade stand in front of his house, hoping to sell his refreshing drinks to thirsty passersby. However, he soon found out that there was a lot of competition in the neighborhood, and he needed to find a way to stand out. That's when he got the idea to make his lemonade stand into a "DIY" experience. He set up a table with different flavors of lemonade and a variety of toppings, like sliced fruit and candy. He even provided instructions on how to mix and match the flavors to create your own unique drink. Kids and adults alike were intrigued by Little David's unique lemonade stand and the challenge of creating their own tasty concoctions. He also created PREMIUM LEMONADE, which was using FRESH Organic ingredient and shake them as normally we do for Cocktail! Before he knew it, he was making more money than he ever had before!

But Little David didn't stop there. He continued to think outside the box and come up with new ways to earn money. As he grew more successful, Little David learned important lessons about money management, saving for the future, and taking calculated risks. He also discovered the joy of being his own boss and doing something he loved while making a profit. Through hard work, determination, and a little bit of fun, Little David proved that anyone – no matter how small – could learn to earn money and achieve their dreams. And who knows? Maybe one day he'll become a successful entrepreneur and inspire others to follow in his footsteps!

Through it all, Little David's spirit of adventure and willingness to take on new challenges made his story a true thrill ride. **Who knows where his entrepreneurial spirit will take him next – but one thing's for sure, he's definitely one to watch! But will his hard work pay off in the end? Will Little David finally get the toy of his dreams, or will he discover that the real treasure was the lessons he learned along the way?** Find out in this heart-warming and hilarious story of one boy's journey from pocket money to financial independence. Will Little David be able to navigate these challenges and achieve his financial goals? Only time will tell, but one thing's for sure – this little boy is on a mission to learn how to earn a lot of money like a pro!

With the help from his parents & family and his teachers also his friends, Little David knew about the basic money concept and money management.

After you buy this book, if you want to, we will send several images about The Interactive Money Management, such as The Sinking Fund, The Money Tracking, Budgeting, Invoice and more to your email. So your children will be able to play and exercise with money management. Please send an email to ask about this request to: theblessedcreation17@gmail.com.

CHAPTER 1

Little David Gets His First Pocket Money Not for His Candy but for His Saving

After he overheard his parents talking about how they struggled to make ends meet and how important it was to save money for the future, Little David was surprised and a little scared by this news, as he had never really thought about money beyond spending it on himself. So Little David felt a newfound sense of responsibility and for his dream to own the latest version of The Electronic Toys, Little David decided to learn how to earn his own money. He asked his teachers, his parents and family, also his friends about basic money concepts and his mission to find ways to increase his pocket money and become more financially independent.

So David learned a lot of things, such as

1. What money is: What coins and notes look like, what they're called and that they're different (and why).He used actual coins and notes in games he played together so he started recognising them and understood about their value too.

2. Understanding that we use money to buy things: This becomes more meaningful when his parents give him the money to hand over to the checkout assistant during a shopping trip. So he understood we don't get something for nothing.

3. He understood that sometime he has to wait before he buy something: Patience and waiting – two things most young children struggle with. When it comes to money though, it's important that he

begin to realise he can't always buy what he want, when he want. Sometimes he has to save, and that takes time.

4. He get money by working: The first step he understood the value of money doesn't simply appear. He knew finally about how we earn money, by going out to work for example, was a great starting point.

5. Money should be kept somewhere safe: His parent help him to set up a bank account and talk about money needing to be kept secure.

6. Earning money: His parents changed about the pocket money. Pocket money was given as a reward for completing chores or other tasks. It helps Little David realise that he need to earn money rather than expecting it to be handed to him.

7. Saving up is important: Little David understood that setting a savings goal for something he really want. This encourages him to cut down spontaneous spending in favour of sensible saving. Help Little David to figure out how long it will take him to save for something. It's a great motivation to help him work towards his goal.

8. Different ways to pay for things: He understood that cash isn't always exchanged when something is purchased. He learned from his parents about how to use credit and debit cards. His parents showed him that the money has gone out of his parents account as a result. So he understood about the concept of 'invisible' money and its value. Seeing what happens to money in his parent bank account before and after something's been paid for really helps.

Little David was a curious and cheerful boy who loved to learn new things. He liked to read books, play games, and explore the world around him. He had many friends at school and at home, and he always tried to be kind and helpful to everyone.

One day, Little David's parents gave him a surprise. They handed him a small envelope with his name on it.

"What's this?" Little David asked, opening the envelope.

"It's your NEW pocket money," his mother said. "We decided that you're old enough to have some money of your own."

Little David looked inside the envelope and saw five shiny coins. He counted them: one, two, three, four and five. Total 5 dollars! He felt a surge of excitement and joy.

"Wow! Thank you so much!" he exclaimed, hugging his parents. "This is awesome!"

His father smiled and ruffled his hair. "You're welcome, son. But remember, this is not the usual gift which normally we gave you weekly. This is money that you earned by doing your chores and being a good boy."

"That's right," his mother added. "And we expect you to use it wisely and responsibly."

David nodded eagerly. He knew what his parents meant. Currently he had learned about money at school and from his friends. He knew that money was something that people used to buy things they wanted or needed. He also knew that money was not easy to come by, and that people had to work hard to earn it. He felt proud of himself for earning his first NEW pocket money. He wondered what he could do with it. He had so many ideas and wishes in his mind. Maybe he could buy a new book from the library. Or maybe he could buy some candy from the store. Or maybe he could save it for something bigger and better. He decided to think about it later. For now, he just wanted to enjoy his NEW pocket money and show it to his friends. He put the envelope in his backpack and ran outside to play. He couldn't wait to tell everyone about his NEW pocket money. He felt like he had just entered a new and exciting world.

Little David did not know that this first NEW pocket money would also lead him to some amazing adventures and discoveries. He would soon learn how to earn more money from his NEW pocket money, how to spend it wisely, how to save it for the future, and how to share it with others. He would also learn some important lessons about life, such as the value of hard work, the joy of generosity, the power of creativity, and the importance of gratitude. He would meet new friends, face new challenges, and have lots of fun along the way. And he would discover that money was not just something that you could buy things with. It was also something that you could learn from, grow from, and make a difference with.

CHAPTER 11

Little David Learns About Saving and Spending

Little David was having a great time with his NEW pocket money. He showed it to his friends at school and they were all impressed.

"Wow, you're rich!" his best friend Sam said.

"Not really," Little David said modestly. "It's just five dollars."

"That's a lot of money," his friend Mia said. "You can buy so many things with it."

"Like what?" Little David asked.

"Well, you can buy a new book from the library," Sam suggested.

"Or you can buy some candy from the store," Mia added.

"Or you can buy a toy car or a doll," another friend said.

Little David thought about all the things he could buy with his NEW pocket money. He liked books, candy, and toys. He wanted to buy them all.

But then he remembered what his parents had told him. They had said that he should use his money wisely and responsibly. They had also said that he should save some of it for the future.

Little David wondered what that meant. How could he use his money wisely and responsibly? How could he save some of it for the future?

He decided to ask his teacher for some advice.

He raised his hand and waited for his teacher to notice him.

"Yes, David?" his teacher asked.

"Can I ask you something?" Little David said.

"Sure, what is it?" his teacher said.

Little David took out his envelope with his pocket money and showed it to his teacher.

"I got this from my parents," he said. "They said it's my NEW pocket money. They said I earned it by doing my chores and being a good boy."

"That's wonderful," his teacher said. "You must be very proud of yourself."

"I am," Little David said. "But I don't know what to do with it. My friends told me I can buy many things with it. But my parents told me I should use it wisely and responsibly. They also told me I should save some of it for the future. What does that mean?"

His teacher smiled and nodded. He understood Little David's dilemma.

"Well, David, your parents are right. You should use your money wisely and responsibly. And you should save some of it for the future."

"But how do I do that?" Little David asked.

His teacher thought for a moment. Then he had an idea.

He took out a piece of paper and a pen from his desk. He drew a circle on the paper and divided it into three parts.

He labeled one part "Saving", another part "Spending", and the last part "Sharing".

He showed the paper to David.

"This is called a money plan," he said. "It's a way of managing your money so that you can use it wisely and responsibly."

He pointed to the part labeled "Saving".

"This is where you put some of your money aside for the future. You can save it for something big or important that you want or need later on. For example, you can save it for college, or for a trip, or for an emergency."

He pointed to the part labeled "Spending".

"This is where you use some of your money to buy things that you want or need now. You can spend it on things that make you happy or help you learn or grow. For example, you can spend it on books, candy, or toys."

He pointed to the part labeled "Sharing".

"This is where you give some of your money to others who need it more than you do. You can share it with people who are less fortunate or who are doing good things in the world. For example, you can share it with a charity, or with a friend, or with your family."

He looked at David and smiled.

"Do you understand?" he asked.

Little David nodded slowly. He looked at the paper and tried to imagine how he would divide his pocket money into three parts.

He thought about saving some of it for something big or important in the future.

He thought about spending some of it on things that made him happy or helped him learn or grow.

He thought about sharing some of it with others who needed it more than him.

He felt a warm feeling in his heart.

He realized that his NEW pocket money was not just something that he could buy things with.

It was also something that he could learn from, grow from, and make a difference with.

Then his teacher told him a bit more about some tips that can help Little David save money:

1. Discuss wants vs. needs: Teaching him the value of saving to distinguish between wants and needs. This help Little David prioritize his spending and save money.
2. Encourage Little David to earn his own money: Little David can earn money by doing chores around the house or by starting

a small business like selling lemonade.

3. Set savings goals: Little David can set a savings goal for his electronic toy and work towards it. This can help him stay motivated and focused.

4. Provide a place to save: Little David can have a piggy bank or a savings account where he can keep his money safe.

5. Have them track spending: Little David can keep track of his spending to see where his money is going and identify areas where he can cut back.

6. Offer savings incentives: His teacher told Little David that his parents or grandparents may offer him an incentives for saving money, like matching his savings or giving him a bonus for reaching his savings goal.

7. Leave room for mistakes: It's important to know that we may make mistakes with our money so we can learn from that mistakes.

8. Act as his creditor: His teacher told Little David, if he need to buy something but doesn't have enough money, his parents or grandparents may lend him the money and charge him interest. This teach Little David about borrowing and interest.

CHAPTER lll

Little David Wants to Buy a New Toy

Little David had been saving his pocket money for months to buy the new electronic toy he had been dreaming of. He had finally saved enough money to buy the toy, but when he went to the store, he realized that the toy was more expensive than he thought. He was disappointed. Little David can do a few things to get the toy he wants. He can save his NEW pocket money for a few weeks or months until he has enough money to buy the toy. He can also ask his parents if they would be willing to give him an advance on his allowance or if he can do extra chores around the house to earn more money. Another option is to sell some of his old toys or items he no longer needs to raise money for the new toy.

As he was walking home, he saw a sign in a store window that said "Help Wanted". Little David went inside and asked if they needed any help. The store owner said that he could use some help stocking shelves and cleaning up around the store. Little David worked hard and earned some extra money. After a few weeks of working at the store, Little David had saved money to buy the toy he wanted. He was so happy and proud of himself for working hard and earning the money he needed, but his money was still not enough to buy the new version of The Electronic Toy.

When he went home and told his mom about his problem. His mom said "Don't worry, Little David. There are lots of ways to earn money. You just have to be creative."

Little David thought about what his mom said and came up with some ideas. He decided to have a yard sale and sell some of his old toys and clothes that he didn't need anymore. He also decided to do some extra chores around the house to earn more money.

He worked hard and saved up enough money to buy the toy he wanted. He was so happy and proud of himself for working hard and earning the money he needed. But again, his money was still not enough to buy the new version of The Electronic Toy. So Little David did so many others jobs such as:

1. Sell crafts online: Little David can make crafts like bracelets, necklaces, or keychains and sell them online with help from his Mom.
2. Do yard work for neighbors: Little David mowed lawns, raked leaves, or did other yard work for his neighbors.
3. Pet-sit for neighbors: Little David took care of his neighbors' pets while they were away.
4. Wash cars: Little David washed cars for his neighbors.
5. Did odd jobs around the house: Little David did some extra chores around the house for his parents or other family members.

But again, his money was still not enough to buy the new version of The Electronic Toy.

CHAPTER IV

Little David Visits His Grandma's Farm

LITTLE DAVID WAS EXCITED to visit his grandma's farm. He had heard so many stories about the farm and all the animals that lived there. He was also hoping to get some ideas about how to earn more money to buy the electronic toy he had been dreaming of.

When he arrived at the farm, his grandma greeted him with a big hug. She showed him around the farm and introduced him to all the animals. There were cows, pigs, chickens, and even a horse!

Little David was fascinated by all the animals and asked his grandma if he could help take care of them. His grandma said "Of course! There's always work to be done on the farm."

Little David spent the day helping his grandma with the animals. He fed the cows and pigs, collected eggs from the chickens, and even helped brush the horse. He worked hard and had a lot of fun.

At the end of the day, Little David sat down with his grandma and told her about his dream of buying the electronic toy. His grandma listened carefully and said "Well, Little David, you're already doing something that can help you earn more money. You're working hard and helping others. That's a great way to earn money."

Little David thought about what his grandma said and realized that she was right. He didn't need to find a special way to earn money. He just needed to work hard and help others.

So the next day, Little David planted and harvested vegetables and fruits from the trees in the garden. He also helped his grandma feed and take care of the animals on the farm. He fixed things around the farm that needed to be repaired. He learned new skills from his grandma, like how to milk a cow and how to make a great cheese as well.

Little David set a savings goal for his electronic toy and worked towards it. He had a piggy bank where he kept his money safe. He tracked his spending to see where his money was going and identified areas where he could cut back.

Sometimes Little David made mistakes with his money, but he learned from them. His parents or grandparents offered incentives for saving money, like matching his savings or giving him a bonus for reaching his savings goal.

Little David faced some challenges along the way. Sometimes he got tired from working on the farm all day, but he didn't give up. He stayed motivated and focused on his goal.

CHAPTER V

Little David Helps with the Chores

Little David was a cheerful and curious boy who loved to explore the world around him, but he also wanted to help his parents with the chores.

One day, he decided to surprise his mom by doing some of the chores while she was busy with the baby. He put on his apron and his gloves and went to the kitchen. He saw a pile of dirty dishes in the sink and thought, "I can wash these dishes for mom. She will be so happy!" He turned on the faucet and filled the sink with water and soap. He picked up a plate and started to scrub it with a sponge. He was very careful not to break it or drop it. He rinsed it and put it on the drying rack. He felt proud of himself and continued with the rest of the dishes.

He was almost done when he heard a loud crash behind him. He turned around and saw that his baby sister had crawled into the kitchen and knocked over a vase of flowers. The vase was broken and the water and the petals were all over the floor. Little David gasped and ran to his sister. He picked her up and checked if she was hurt. Luckily, she was not hurt, but she was crying. Little David tried to calm her down by singing a lullaby. He carried her to the living room and put her on the couch. He gave her a toy to play with and covered her with a blanket. He thought, "I need to clean up the mess in the kitchen before mom sees it. She will be so angry!"

He ran back to the kitchen and grabbed a mop and a dustpan. He swept up the broken pieces of the vase and threw them in the trash. He mopped up the water and the petals from the floor. He wiped the table and the counter with a cloth. He finished washing the dishes and put them away in the cupboard. He looked around and saw that the kitchen was sparkling clean. He felt proud of himself again and thought, "I did a good job! Mom will be so happy!"

He went back to the living room and saw that his baby sister had fallen asleep on the couch. He smiled and kissed her on the forehead. He thought, "I love my sister. She is so cute!" He heard his mom coming down the stairs. He ran to her and hugged her. He said, "Mom, I have a surprise for you! I did some of the chores for you!"

His mom looked surprised and curious. She said, "You did? What did you do?" Little David took her by the hand and showed her the kitchen. He said, "Look, mom! I washed all the dishes for you! And I cleaned up the mess that my sister made when she broke your vase!" His mom looked at him with love and admiration. She said, "Wow, David! You did all that by yourself? You are such a big boy! You are such a good helper! Thank you so much!"

She hugged him and kissed him on the cheek. She said, "You made me very happy today, David! I'm so proud of you!"

Little David felt happy too. He said, "You're welcome, mom! I'm glad I could help you! I love you!"

They hugged each other again and went to check on his baby sister. They cuddled with her on the couch and read a story together.

Little David learned that helping with the chores can be fun and rewarding. He decided to help his mom more often from then on.

Another day, he decided to surprise his dad by doing some of the laundry while he was at work. He put on his apron and his gloves and went to the laundry room. He saw a basket of dirty clothes and thought, "I can wash these clothes for dad. He will be so happy!"

He turned on the washing machine and put some detergent in it. He sorted the clothes by color and put them in the machine. He closed the lid and pressed the start button. He watched the clothes spin and get clean. He thought, "This is fun! I wonder how the dryer works."

He waited for the washing machine to finish and then opened the lid. He took out the wet clothes and put them in the dryer. He closed the door and pressed the start button. He watched the clothes tumble and get dry. He thought, "This is easy! I wonder how to fold them?"

He waited for the dryer to finish and then opened the door. He took out the dry clothes and put them on a table. He tried to fold them neatly like his dad did. He folded shirts, pants, socks, and underwear. He made a pile for each family member. He thought, "This is hard! But I can do it!"

He finished folding all the clothes and put them in a basket. He carried the basket to his parents' bedroom and put it on their bed. He arranged the clothes nicely and left a note that said, "I did the laundry for you! Love, David."

He looked at his work and felt proud of himself. He thought, "I did a good job! Dad will be so happy!"

He went back to the laundry room and cleaned up the mess. He put away the detergent and the gloves. He wiped the machines with a cloth.

He heard his dad coming home from work. He ran to him and hugged him. He said, "Dad, I have a surprise for you! I did some of the chores for you!"

His dad looked surprised and curious. He said, what did you do?"

Little David took him by the hand and showed him their bedroom. He said, "Look, dad! I washed all your clothes for you! And I folded them too!"

His dad looked at him with love and gratitude. He said, "Wow, David! You did all that by yourself? You are such a big boy! Thank you so much!"

He hugged him and kissed him on the cheek. He said, "You made me very happy today, David! I'm so proud of you!"

Little David felt happy too. He said, "You're welcome, dad! I'm glad I could help you! I love you!"

They hugged each other again and went to check on his mom and his baby sister. They had dinner together and watched a movie.

Little David learned that helping with the laundry can be fun and rewarding.

Little David did another chores for his parents, such as:

- Water the garden and indoor plants
- Feed pets
- Help with hanging out clothes and folding washing
- Take out rubbish
- Help with choosing meals and shopping
- Help with meal preparation and serving, under supervision
- Vacuum or sweep floors
- Clean the bathroom sink, wipe down kitchen benches, or mop floors.

- Making bed independently
- Dusting
- Helping out to cook and prepare food
- Carrying and putting away groceries
- Sorting laundry whites and colors

CHAPTER VI

Little David Earns His First and His Second Extra Money

ONE DAY, LITTLE DAVID decided to visit the old bookstore near his house. He had never been inside before, but he had heard that it was full of rare and interesting books. He walked into the store and was greeted by a friendly old man who was the owner.

"Hello there, young man. What can I do for you?" the old man asked.

"I'm just looking around. I love books," Little David said.

"Well, you've come to the right place. This store has books from all over the world and from all kinds of genres. Feel free to browse as much as you like," the old man said.

Little David thanked him and started to look at the shelves. He was amazed by the variety of books he saw. There were books about history, science, art, magic, mystery, adventure and more. He picked up a few books and read the summaries on the back covers. He was especially drawn to a book about pirates and another one about dinosaurs.

He wanted to buy both books, but he realized that he didn't have any money with him. He felt sad and wondered if he could ever afford them.

"Excuse me, sir. How much are these books?" he asked the old man.

The old man looked at the books and smiled.

"Those are two of my favorites. They are very rare and valuable. They cost $10 each," he said.

Little David felt his heart sink. He knew that he didn't have that much money. He wondered if he could ask his parents for some allowance, but he knew that they were struggling financially and couldn't spare any extra money.

He sighed and put the books back on the shelf.

"I'm sorry, sir. I can't buy them. I don't have any money," he said.

The old man noticed his disappointment and felt sorry for him.

"Don't be sad, young man. I have an idea. How about you help me out with some chores around the store and I'll pay you $10 for each hour of work? That way, you can earn enough money to buy the books you want," he offered.

Little David's eyes lit up. He liked the idea of working for his own money and being able to buy the books he wanted.

"Really? You would do that for me?" he asked.

"Of course. You seem like a smart and hardworking boy. I could use some help around here. It's not easy running this store by myself," the old man said.

"Thank you so much, sir. I would love to help you," Little David said.

"Great. Then let's get started. Follow me," the old man said.

He led Little David to the back of the store where there were boxes of books that needed to be sorted and shelved. He explained to Little David how to organize them by genre and alphabetically by author's name.

Little David nodded and got to work. He enjoyed sorting through the books and learning about different topics. He also liked talking to the old man who told him stories about his travels and his experiences as a bookstore owner.

They worked together for two hours until Little David had sorted and shelved all the boxes of books.

"Wow, you did a great job, young man. You're very fast and efficient," the old man praised him.

"Thank you, sir. It was fun," Little David said.

"Well, you've earned your money fair and square. Here you go," the old man said as he handed Little David a $20 bill.

Little David took the money and thanked him again.

"Now you can buy those books you wanted," the old man said.

"Yes, I can! Thank you so much for this opportunity, sir. You're very kind," Little David said.

He ran back to the shelf where he had seen the pirate and dinosaur books and picked them up. He was so happy that he could finally buy them.

He went to the counter where the old man rang up his purchase.

"Here you go, young man. Enjoy your books," the old man said as he handed Little David a receipt.

"Thank you, sir. I will," Little David said as he hugged his books close to his chest.

He waved goodbye to the old man and left the store with a big smile on his face.

He had earned his first extra money and bought his first books with it.

Another day, Little David decided to set up a small stand outside his house and sell his drawings to the people passing by. He thought that it would be a fun way to make some extra money and also make some new friends.

He asked his parents for permission and they agreed. They helped him make a sign that said "David's Art Gallery" and gave him some change to make change for his customers.

He took his sketchbook and some pencils and crayons and went outside. He set up his stand on the sidewalk and waited for customers.

He didn't have to wait long. Soon, a woman with a dog stopped by and looked at his drawings.

"Wow, these are beautiful. Did you draw them yourself?" she asked.

"Yes, I did. Thank you," Little David said.

"I love this one of the dog. It looks just like mine. How much is it?" she asked.

"It's $1," Little David said.

"That's very reasonable. I'll take it," she said as she handed Little David a dollar bill.

Little David thanked her and gave her the drawing. He also gave her a receipt that he had made with his name and address on it.

"Thank you for buying my drawing. I hope you like it," Little David said.

"I'm sure I will. It's very cute. Keep up the good work," she said as she smiled and walked away with her dog.

Little David was very happy. He had made his first sale.

He continued to sell his drawings to other people who stopped by his stand. He sold drawings of cats, birds, flowers, cars and more. He made $10 in total.

He was very proud of himself. He had earned his first extra money and sold his first drawings with it.

After so many weeks hard work to earn money to buy The Latest Version of Electronic Toy, today Little David decided for not spending his money to buy this toy. Little David agreed with his Parents, Grandma, his teacher and friends to use his money for other more useful later.

CHAPTER VII

Little David Meets His Cousin Lily

Little David was excited to meet his cousin Lily for the first time. He had heard a lot about her from his parents and grandparents. She was the same age as him and lived in another city. She was coming to visit him for a week during the summer holidays. Little David waited eagerly at the airport with his parents. He held a sign that said "Welcome Lily" that he had made himself. He wondered what she looked like and what she liked to do.

Soon, he saw a girl with long blonde hair and blue eyes walking towards them with a suitcase. She was wearing a pink dress and a matching hat. She looked very pretty and cheerful.

She saw Little David and his parents and waved at them.

"Hi, I'm Lily. You must be David," she said as she hugged him.

"Hi, I'm David. It's nice to meet you," Little David said.

They smiled at each other and felt an instant connection.

They got into the car and drove to David's house. They chatted along the way and found out that they had a lot in common. They both liked to read, draw, play games and watch movies.

They reached David's house and went inside. Little David showed Lily his room and his toys. He also showed her his sketchbook where he kept his drawings.

"Wow, you're very good at drawing. I like this one of the cat," Lily said as she pointed at one of David's drawings.

"Thank you. I love to draw. I sell my drawings sometimes to people who pass by my house," David said.

"Really? That's so cool. How much do you charge for them?" Lily asked.

"I charge $1 for each drawing. I've made $10 so far," David said proudly.

"That's amazing. You're very smart and talented," Lily said.

"Thank you. Do you have any hobbies?" Little David asked.

"I like to sing and dance. I take lessons every week. I also like to make bracelets and necklaces with beads and strings," Lily said.

"That sounds fun. Do you sell them too?" Little David asked.

"No, I don't. I just make them for myself and my friends," Lily said.

"Why don't you sell them? You could make some extra money too," Little David suggested.

"I don't know. I never thought about it. Do you think people would buy them?" Lily asked.

"Sure, they would. They're very pretty and colorful. You could sell them for $2 or $3 each," Little David said.

"Really? That sounds like a good idea. Maybe I'll try it," Lily said.

They decided to make some bracelets and necklaces together and sell them outside David's house the next day. They had a lot of fun making them and choosing different beads and strings.

The next day, they set up a small stand on the sidewalk and displayed their creations. They made a sign that said "Lily and David's Jewelry Shop".

They waited for customers and soon they had some. People liked their bracelets and necklaces and bought them for themselves or as gifts for others.

They sold all of their jewelry in an hour and made $20 in total.

They were very happy. They had earned some extra money and had fun doing it.

The next day, David showed Lily his piggy bank where he kept his money. "Wow, you have a lot of money in there. How did you get it?" Lily asked. "I saved it from my allowance and from doing chores around the house. I also sold some of my old toys and books that I didn't need anymore," David said.

"That's very impressive. You're very responsible and thrifty," Lily said.

"Thank you. Do you have any money?" Little David asked.

"I do. I have some money in my bank account that I earned from doing different things," Lily said.

"Like what?" David asked.

"Well, I like to write stories and poems. I have a blog where I post them and sometimes people pay me to write for them or to read their work and give them feedback," Lily said.

"Wow, that's awesome. You're very creative and skilled," Little David said.

"Thank you. I also like to bake cookies and cakes. I have a small business where I sell them to my neighbors and friends. They're very popular and delicious," Lily said.

"That sounds yummy. You're very entrepreneurial and talented," David said.

"Thank you. Do you want to try some? I brought some with me in my backpack," Lily offered.

"Sure, I'd love to," David said.

They went to the kitchen and Lily took out a box of cookies and a cake from her backpack. She gave some to David and his parents.

They tasted them and they were indeed very good.

"Mmm, these are amazing. You're a great baker, Lily," David's mom said.

"Thank you. I'm glad you like them," Lily said.

They ate the cookies and cake and talked more about their hobbies and interests. They found out that they had some things in common.

They decided to play chess together and watch some cartoons on TV. They also taught each other some words in their languages.

They had a lot of fun and became more comfortable with each other.

They realized that they were not so different after all.

They had earned some money and had fun doing it.

CHAPTER VIII
Little David Learns About Budgeting

LITTLE DAVID WAS A smart and hardworking boy who liked to earn and save money. He had a piggy bank where he kept his money from his allowance, chores and selling his drawings. He also had a wish list of things he wanted to buy with his money. One day, he decided to count his money and see how much he had. He took out his piggy bank and emptied it on his bed. He counted the coins and bills and wrote down the total amount on a piece of paper.

He had $50 in total. He was very happy. He thought that he had enough money to buy everything on his wish list.

He took out his wish list and looked at it. It had five items on it:

- A new bike ($100)
- A video game ($40)
- A book ($10)
- A toy car ($5)
- A candy bar ($1)

He added up the prices of the items and wrote down the total amount on another piece of paper.

He had $156 in total.

He was very confused. He thought that he had enough money to buy everything on his wish list, but he didn't. He had less money than he needed.

He wondered what he did wrong and how he could fix it.

He decided to ask his mom for help. He went to the kitchen where his mom was making dinner.

"Mom, can I ask you something?" he said.

"Sure, honey. What is it?" his mom said.

"I have a problem with my money. I counted it and I have $50, but I want to buy things that cost $156. How can I do that?" he asked.

His mom smiled and hugged him.

"That's a good question, honey. You're very smart to want to learn about money. Let me explain something to you. It's called budgeting," she said.

"What's budgeting?" David asked.

"Budgeting is a way of planning how to spend your money wisely. It helps you to save money for the things you want and need, and to avoid spending more than you have," she said.

"How do you do that?" David asked.

"Well, there are some important factors in budgeting that you need to know. The first one is income," she said.

"What's income?" David asked.

"Income is the money that you earn or receive from different sources. For example, your allowance, your chores and your drawings are your income sources," she said.

"Oh, I see. So my income is $50," David said.

"That's right. The second factor is expenses," she said.

"What's expenses?" David asked.

"Expenses are the money that you spend or need to spend on different things. For example, your wish list items are your expenses," she said.

"Oh, I see. So my expenses are $156," David said.

"That's right. The third factor is savings," she said.

"What's savings?" David asked.

"Savings are the money that you keep or put aside for future use. For example, your piggy bank is your savings," she said.

"Oh, I see. So my savings are $0," David said sadly.

"That's okay, honey. You can always increase your savings by earning more income or spending less expenses," she said.

"How do I do that?" David asked eagerly.

"Well, there are some tips that can help you with that. The first tip is to set a goal," she said.

"What's a goal?" David asked.

"A goal is something that you want to achieve or accomplish with your money. For example, buying a new bike can be your goal," she said.

"Oh, I see. So my goal is to buy a new bike," David said.

"That's right. The second tip is to make a plan," she said.

"What's a plan?" David asked.

"A plan is a way of organizing your income, expenses and savings to reach your goal. For example, you can write down how much money you need for your goal, how much money you have now, how much money you can earn or save each week or month, and how long it will take you to reach your goal," she said.

"Oh, I see. So I need to make a plan for buying a new bike," David said.

"That's right. The third tip is to track your progress," she said.

"What's progress?" David asked.

"Progress is the amount of money that you have earned or saved towards your goal. For example, you can use a chart or a jar to show how much money you have now and how much more you need for your goal," she explained.

"Oh, I see. So I need to track my progress for buying a new bike," David said.

"That's right. The fourth tip is to be flexible," she said.

"What's flexible?" David asked.

"Flexible means being able to adjust or change your plan if something unexpected happens. For example, if you earn more or less money than you expected, or if the price of your goal changes, or if you find something else that you want to buy, you can change your plan accordingly," she said.

"Oh, I see. So I need to be flexible for buying a new bike," David said.

"That's right. The fifth and final tip is to celebrate your success," she said.

"What's success?" David asked.

"Success means achieving or accomplishing your goal. For example, when you have enough money to buy your new bike, you can celebrate by buying it and enjoying it," she said.

"Oh, I see. So I need to celebrate my success for buying a new bike," David said.

"That's right. Do you understand everything I've told you?" she asked.

"I think so. Budgeting is a way of planning how to spend my money wisely. It has income, expenses and savings as factors. It has goal, plan, progress, flexibility and success as tips. It helps me to save money for the things I want and need, and to avoid spending more than I have," David summarized.

"That's very good, honey. You're very smart and quick to learn. I'm proud of you," she said.

"Thank you, mom. You're very kind and helpful. I love you," he said.

"I love you too, honey. Now let's make a plan for buying your new bike together," she said.

They went to David's room and took out a piece of paper and a pencil. They wrote down David's goal, income, expenses and savings. They calculated how much money he needed for his goal, how much money he had now, how much money he could earn or save each week or month, and how long it would take him to reach his goal.

They made a chart to track his progress and a jar to collect his savings. They also agreed to be flexible if anything changed along the way.

They were very happy. They had learned about budgeting and made a plan for buying a new bike.

Note for parents, about Teaching Budgeting to your children:

A. MAKE IT FUN:

Budgeting is part of our daily money management, so please make it part of your children as well. Our children learn from us and they love playing games, so we combine the two. Shopping games are great for our children, both real and make-believe. So we create a shopping list, look at the price of each item, then add the prices up AND compare the total with what we have actually got in our wallet. With this, our children will realise that everything has a cost and sometimes they may not be able to afford what they want to buy. Once they understand about this, it is a great idea to introduce budgeting to them. Budgeting will be one of the most useful skills our children will ever learn.

B. KEEEP TRACK:

Tracking the money, it is the key to great budgeting. Knowing how much money is in their money box or in their bank account and what's left when they take money out is the great starting point. After our children understand about this concept, we could introduce the idea of setting a saving goal, so our children will get a sense of forward planning and start estimating how much money they need to save up to buy something.

C. SET A SAVINGS GOAL:

Our children may have an idea of what something costs, but they may not have a clue how much they need to save to buy it. So now, this is a time to set a savings goal. So our children will set a certain amount of money aside each week, and how many weeks it will take before they can afford their goal.

D. TEACH THEM THE IMPLICATION OF OVER-SPENDING:

There is a time, when our children spend all their pocket money, meaning they can't buy something as a result. This is a very important lesson in itself. Do not bail them out, because it will not help them in the long-run. Please explain to our children that what they could do differently next time. Please introduce the idea of comparing prices (so they can buy the cheaper one) and what they can do to earn more pocket money. If our children want to learn about budgeting, they need to take control of their money. Our children should know, what money they have got, what they are spending it on, how they can earn more are important stepping stones towards developing strong savings and budgeting skills.

CHAPTER IX
Little David Goes To the Market

Little David was a curious and adventurous boy who liked to learn new things. He had a notebook where he wrote down his ideas for earning more money.

One day, he decided to go to the market and do a market survey. He wanted to get an idea of what people liked to buy and sell, and how much they charged or paid for different things. He thought that it would help him to come up with a good product or service to offer. He asked his mom for permission and she agreed. She gave him some money to buy something for himself and some snacks for them. She also gave him a map of the market and told him to be careful and come back before dark.

He thanked her and took his piggy bank, his notebook, his pencil and his backpack. He walked to the market and entered through the main gate.

He was amazed by the sights, sounds and smells of the market. There were stalls and shops selling all kinds of things, such as fruits, vegetables, flowers, clothes, toys, books, jewelry and more. There were also people offering different services, such as haircuts, massages, repairs, portraits and more. He decided to start from one end of the market and work his way to the other. He looked at each stall and shop carefully and wrote down what they sold or offered, how much they charged or paid, how many customers they had, and what made them unique or attractive.

He also talked to some of the sellers and buyers and asked them questions about their products or services, their preferences, their opinions and their suggestions.

He learned a lot from his market survey. He found out that some things were more popular or profitable than others, such as fresh fruits and vegetables, handmade crafts, personalized items and entertainment services. He also found out that some things were more important or appealing than others, such as quality, variety, price, convenience and customer service.

He also bought some things for himself and some snacks for his mom. He bought a banana for 25 cents, a comic book for $2, a bracelet with his name on it for $5 and a bag of popcorn for $1.

He spent $8.25 in total.

He was very happy. He had done a market survey and got an idea for earning money.

CHAPTER X
Little David Learns About Investing

Little David was a smart and hardworking boy who liked to earn and save money. One day, he decided to learn about investing. He wanted to get an idea of how to make his money grow and work for him. He thought that it would help him to achieve his financial goals faster and easier. He asked his dad for help. His dad was an investor and knew a lot about investing.

"Dad, can you teach me about investing?" he asked.

"Sure, son. I'm happy to teach you about investing. Investing is a way of putting your money into something that can increase in value over time. For example, you can invest your money in shares, which are small pieces of ownership in a company. When you buy shares, you become a part-owner of that company and you can benefit from its profits and growth," his dad explained.

"Wow, that sounds cool. How do I buy shares?" David asked.

"Well, you need to open an investment account first. There are different types of investment accounts for kids, such as minor's accounts or trust accounts. They have different rules and benefits, so you need to do some research and find out what suits you best. You also need to have a tax file number and quote it when you open your account," his dad said.

"Okay, I'll look into that. What else do I need to know?" David asked.

"You also need to know how to choose which shares to buy. There are thousands of companies that you can invest in, but not all of them are good investments. You need to do some research and analysis on the companies that interest you and find out their financial performance, growth potential, competitive advantage and risks. You also need to diversify your portfolio, which means buying shares from different companies and industries to reduce your risk," his dad said.

"Wow, that sounds complicated. How do I do that?" David asked.

"Well, you can use different sources of information, such as websites, books, magazines, newsletters and podcasts to learn more about the companies and the share market. You can also use online tools and calculators to compare and evaluate different shares. You can also ask for advice from experts or professionals if you need help," his dad said.

"Okay, I'll try that. How much money do I need to start investing?" David asked.

"Well, that depends on how much you can afford and how much the shares cost. Some shares are more expensive than others, but you don't have to buy a whole share. You can buy a fraction of a share with as little as $5. You can also use dollar-cost averaging, which means investing a fixed amount of money at regular intervals regardless of the share price. This can help you reduce the impact of market fluctuations and lower your average cost per share," his dad said.

"Okay, I think I understand. Thank you for teaching me about investing, dad," David said.

"You're welcome, son. I'm proud of you for wanting to learn about investing. Investing is a great way to make your money grow and work for you," his dad said.

They hugged each other and decided to open an investment account for David together.

The next day, when his Dad was in his office, Little David asked his mom for help. His mom was an entrepreneur and knew a lot about investing.

"Mom, can you teach me about investing?" he asked.

"Sure, honey. I'm happy to teach you about investing. Investing is a way of using your money to create something that can generate income or profit for you. For example, you can invest your money in a business, which is an activity or organization that provides goods or services to customers. When you start or join a business, you can earn money from selling your goods or services to customers," his mom explained.

"Wow, that sounds fun. How do I start or join a business?" David asked.

"Well, you need to have an idea for a business first. There are different types of businesses, such as product-based businesses or service-based businesses. You need to think of something that you are good at or passionate about, and something that people need or want. You also need to do some research and find out who your target market is, what your competitors are doing, and how you can make your business unique or better," his mom said.

"Okay, I'll think about that. What else do I need to know?" David asked.

"You also need to know how to run your business. There are different aspects of running a business, such as planning, budgeting, marketing, selling, delivering and managing. You need to have a clear plan for your business, such as what your goals are, what your strategies are, and what your actions are. You also need to have a budget for your business, such as how much money you need to start and operate your business, how much money you expect to earn and spend, and how much money you want to save or reinvest," his mom said.

"Wow, that sounds complicated. How do I do that?" David asked.

"Well, you can use different resources and tools to help you with running your business, such as websites, books, apps, software and mentors. You can also use different methods and techniques to improve your business, such as testing, measuring, evaluating and adjusting. You can also ask for feedback and support from your customers, partners and advisors if you need help," his mom said.

"Okay, I'll try that. How much money do I need to start or join a business?" David asked.

"Well, that depends on what kind of business you want to start or join. Some businesses require more money than others, but you don't have to spend a lot of money to start or join a business. You can use your own money or borrow money from your family or friends. You can also use crowdfunding or grants to raise money for your business. You can also use bootstrapping or lean startup methods to start or join a business with minimal resources," his mom said.

"Okay, I think I understand. Thank you for teaching me about investing, mom," David said.

"You're welcome, honey. I'm proud of you for wanting to learn about investing. Investing is a great way to use your money wisely and create more value with it," his mom said.

They hugged each other and decided to brainstorm some ideas for David's business together.

CHAPTER XI

Little David Learns About Different Currencies

ONE DAY, HE DECIDED to learn about different currencies that people use in different countries. He asked his mom if he could use her laptop and she said yes. She gave him her laptop and told him to be careful and not to download anything. She also told him to use a website that she had bookmarked for him. Little David opened the laptop and went to the website that his mom had bookmarked. It was a website that had information and pictures of different currencies from around the world. He saw a map of the world and a list of countries. He thought, "Wow! There are so many countries and so many currencies! I wonder what they look like and what they are worth."

He decided to start with the currency that he was familiar with. He clicked on the United States of America on the map and saw a picture of a dollar bill. He saw that it had a number 1 on it and a picture of George Washington. He also saw that it had words like "United States of America", "One Dollar", and "In God We Trust". He thought, "This is the currency that I use every day. It is called the US dollar or USD. It is worth 100 cents or pennies. I can buy things with it at the store or online."

He clicked on another country on the map. He clicked on the United Kingdom and saw a picture of a pound coin. He saw that it had a number 1 on it and a picture of Queen Elizabeth II. He also saw that it had words like "One Pound", "Elizabeth II", and "D G Reg F D". He thought, "This is the currency that they use in the United Kingdom. It is called the pound sterling or GBP. It is worth 100 pence or pennies. I can buy things with it if I go to England or Scotland or Wales or Northern Ireland."

He clicked on another country on the map.

He clicked on Germany and saw a picture of a euro note. He saw that it had a number 5 on it and a picture of a bridge. He also saw that it had words like "Euro", "5", and "BCE ECB EZB EKT EKP". He thought, "This is the currency that they use in Germany and many other countries in Europe. It is called the euro or EUR. It is worth 100 cents or eurocents. I can buy things with it if I go to France or Italy or Spain or Greece or many other countries."

He clicked on another country on the map.

He clicked on Japan and saw a picture of a yen coin. He saw that it had a number 100 on it and a picture of a cherry blossom. He also saw that it had words like "Nippon Ginko", "100", and "Yen". He thought, "This is the currency that they use in Japan. It is called the yen or JPY. It is worth 100 sen or rin. I can buy things with it if I go to Tokyo or Kyoto or Osaka or any other place in Japan."

He clicked on another country on the map. He clicked on China and saw a picture of a yuan note. He saw that it had a number 10 on it and a picture of Mao Zedong. He also saw that it had words like "Zhongguo Renmin Yinhang", "10", and "Yuan". He thought, "This is the currency that they use in China. It is called the yuan or CNY. It is worth 100 fen or jiao. I can buy things with it if I go to Beijing or Shanghai or Hong Kong or any other place in China."

He clicked on another country on the map. He clicked on Australia and saw a picture of an Australian dollar note. He saw that it had a number 10 on it and a picture of Banjo Paterson and Dame Mary Gilmore. He also saw that it had words like "Australia", "10 Dollars", and "Australian". He thought, "This is the currency that they use in Australia.

It is called the Australian dollar or AUD. It is worth 100 cents or pennies. I can buy things with it if I go to Sydney or Melbourne or Brisbane or any other place in Australia."

He clicked on more countries on the map and saw more pictures of different currencies. He saw currencies like the Canadian dollar, the Indian rupee, the Mexican peso, the Brazilian real, and more. He thought, "There are so many currencies in the world! They all look different and have different names and values. I wonder how they compare to each other."

He saw a button on the website that said "Currency Converter". He clicked on it and saw a tool that let him enter an amount of money in one currency and see how much it was worth in another currency. He thought, "This is cool! I can see how much money I have in different currencies!"

He decided to try it out. He entered 10 US dollars and chose to convert it to British pounds. He saw that 10 US dollars was worth about 7.5 British pounds. He thought, "Wow! The pound is stronger than the dollar! That means I can buy less things with the same amount of money in the UK than in the US."

He entered 10 US dollars again and chose to convert it to Japanese yen. He saw that 10 US dollars was worth about 1100 Japanese yen. He thought, "Wow! The yen is weaker than the dollar! That means I can buy more things with the same amount of money in Japan than in the US."

He entered 10 US dollars again and chose to convert it to euros. He saw that 10 US dollars was worth about 9 euros. He thought, "Hmm. The euro is almost equal to the dollar. That means I can buy about the same amount of things with the same amount of money in Europe as in the US."

He entered different amounts of money and different currencies and saw how they changed. He learned that some currencies were stronger or weaker than others and that they changed over time. He also learned that some countries used the same currency as others and that some countries had more than one currency.

He thought, "This is interesting! I learned a lot about different currencies today. I hope I can use them someday when I travel to different countries."

He looked at his watch and saw that it was time for him to go his room. He thought, "I had a great time on this website today. I found a lot of information and pictures of different currencies from around the world. I learned a lot of new things. I hope I can remember them."

He closed the laptop and put it back where he found it. He thanked his mom for letting him use it and told her what he did.

His mom looked at him with love and admiration. She said, "Wow, David! You learned about different currencies today? You are such a big boy! You are such a good explorer! Thank you for telling me what you did!"

She hugged him and kissed him on the cheek. She said, "You made me very happy today, David! I'm so proud of you!"

Little David felt happy too. He said, "You're welcome, mom! I'm glad I could make you happy! I love you!"

They hugged each other again and went to have dinner with his dad and his baby sister.

Little David learned that learning about different currencies can be fun and useful. He decided to learn more about them later.

CHAPTER XII

Little David Learns About Taxes

One day, he decided to learn about taxes that people pay to the government. He asked his dad if he could help him with his taxes and he said yes. He gave him some papers and a calculator and told him to sit with him at the table. He also told him to listen carefully and ask questions if he didn't understand something.

Little David sat with his dad at the table and looked at the papers and the calculator. He saw numbers and words that he didn't know. He thought, "Wow! This looks complicated! I wonder what it all means."

He asked his dad, "Dad, what are taxes?"

His dad smiled and said, "Taxes are money that we pay to the government for the things that they do for us."

He asked his dad, "What kind of things do they do for us?"

His dad said, "They do many things for us. They build roads and bridges and schools and hospitals. They provide police and fire and ambulance services. They protect us from enemies and disasters. They make laws and rules that keep us safe and fair. They help people who are poor or sick or old or in need."

He asked his dad, "Why do we have to pay them money for these things?"

His dad said, "Because these things cost money. The government needs money to pay for the people who work for them and the materials and equipment that they use. The government gets money from different sources, but one of the main sources is taxes."

He asked his dad, "How do they get taxes from us?"

His dad said, "They get taxes from us in different ways. One way is by taking a part of our income or the money that we earn from our jobs or businesses. This is called income tax. Another way is by adding a part of the price of the things that we buy or sell. This is called sales tax. Another way is by charging us a part of the value of the things that we own or use. This is called property tax."

He asked his dad, "How do they know how much tax to take from us?"

His dad said, "They have rules and formulas that tell them how much tax to take from us based on different factors like our income level, our family size, our expenses, our deductions, our credits, and more. These rules and formulas are written in laws that are passed by the people who represent us in the government."

He asked his dad, "How do we know how much tax we have to pay?"

His dad said, "We have to fill out forms that show how much income we made, how much tax we paid already, how much tax we owe or get back, and other information. These forms are called tax returns. We have to send these forms to the government by a certain date every year. This date is called the tax deadline."

He asked his dad, "What happens if we don't pay our taxes or fill out our forms?"

His dad said, "We can get in trouble with the government. They can charge us penalties or interest or fines or fees. They can take away some of our money or property or rights. They can also audit us and check our records and documents for errors or fraud. They can even put us in jail."

Little David said, "That sounds scary!

How can we avoid getting in trouble?"

His dad said, "We can avoid getting in trouble by paying our taxes on time and filling out our forms correctly and honestly. We can also ask for help from people who know more about taxes than we do. These people are called tax preparers or accountants or lawyers."

He asked his dad, "What happens if we pay too much in taxes?"

His dad said, "If we pay too much in taxes, we can get a refund from the government. The government will send us a check or deposit money into our bank account for the amount that we overpaid in taxes. We can use this money for whatever we want."

He asked his dad, "Can you help me with my taxes?"

His dad said, "Of course I can help you with your taxes. You don't have to pay any taxes yet because you are too young and you don't have any income or property. But you can learn about taxes now so that you will be ready when you grow up and have to pay your own taxes."

He asked his dad, "Can you teach me how to fill out these forms?"

His dad said, "Sure I can teach you how to fill out these forms. But first you have to understand some basic concepts and terms that are used in these forms. Let me explain them to you."

His dad explained some basic concepts and terms like gross income, taxable income, adjusted gross income, deductions,

Little David listened to his dad and learned a lot about taxes. He helped his dad fill out the forms and calculate the taxes. He thought, "This is hard! But I can do it!"

He finished helping his dad with his taxes and gave him a hug. He said, "Dad, thank you for teaching me about taxes today!"

His dad hugged him back and said, "You're welcome, Little David! You are such a big boy! You are such a good helper! Thank you for helping me with my taxes today!"

He said, "You made me very happy today, David! I'm so proud of you!"

Little David felt happy too. He said, "You're welcome, dad! I'm glad I could make you happy! I love you!"

They hugged each other again and put away the papers and the calculator. They went to have dinner with his mom and his baby sister.

Little David learned that learning about taxes can be hard but important. He decided to learn more about them later.

CHAPTER XIII
Little David Opens a Bank Account

Little David decided that he needs to open a bank account with his dad. He asked his dad if he could go with him to the bank and he said yes. He gave him some money that he had saved from his allowance and his birthday and told him to put it in his wallet. He also told him to bring his ID card and his social security card.

Little David packed his wallet with his money and his cards. He put on his jacket and his shoes and went outside. He got in the car with his dad and drove to the bank. He thought, "I wonder what it's like to have a bank account. Maybe I can earn interest or get a debit card or use an ATM."

He got to the bank and saw a big sign that said "Welcome to the Bank". He felt excited and entered the bank.

He saw a lot of people and machines in the bank. He saw people who were wearing suits and ties and name tags. They were called bankers or tellers or managers. He saw machines that were called ATMs or cashiers or depositors. They were used to withdraw or deposit or transfer money.

He followed his dad to a counter where a friendly lady was sitting. She had a name tag that said "Miss Smith".

She smiled and said, "Hello, how can I help you today?"

His dad said, "Hello, Miss Smith. We would like to open a bank account for my son, Little David."

Miss Smith said, "Sure, we can do that. Do you have your ID cards and your social security cards with you?"

His dad said, "Yes, we do." He took out his wallet and gave Miss Smith his ID card and his social security card. He also took out Little David's wallet and gave Miss Smith his ID card and his social security card.

Miss Smith scanned their cards and typed something on her computer. She said, "Okay, I have your information here. What kind of account would you like to open for Little David?"

His dad said, "We would like to open a savings account for him. He wants to save his money for the future."

Miss Smith said, "That's a good idea. A savings account is an account where you can deposit your money and earn interest on it. Interest is money that the bank pays you for keeping your money with them. The more money you have in your account, the more interest you earn."

She took out a brochure and showed it to them. It had pictures and words that explained the features and benefits of a savings account. It said things like "No monthly fees", "Free online banking", "Free ATM card", "Minimum balance of $25", "Interest rate of 3.5% per year", and more.

She said, "These are some of the things that you get when you open a savings account with us. Do you have any questions?"

Little David looked at the brochure and asked, "What is a monthly fee?"

Miss Smith said, "A monthly fee is a fee that some banks charge you for having an account with them. They deduct it from your balance every month. But we don't charge you any monthly fees for having a savings account with us."

Little David asked, "What is online banking?"

Miss Smith said, "Online banking is a service that lets you access your account from your computer or your phone or your tablet. You can check your balance, transfer money, pay bills, and more."

Little David asked, "What is an ATM card?"

Miss Smith said, "An ATM card is a card that lets you withdraw or deposit money from your account at any ATM machine. You can also use it to pay for things at some stores or online. You just need to enter your PIN number and follow the instructions on the screen."

Little David asked, "What is a PIN number?"

Miss Smith said, "A PIN number is a personal identification number that you choose when you open your account. It is a secret code that only you know. You need to enter it every time you use your ATM card. It protects your account from unauthorized access or fraud."

Little David asked, "What is a minimum balance?"

Miss Smith said, "A minimum balance is the amount of money that you need to have in your account at all times. If your balance goes below the minimum, you may lose some of the benefits of your account or pay a penalty fee. For a savings account, the minimum balance is $25."

Little David asked, "What is an interest rate?"

Miss Smith said, "An interest rate is the percentage of money that the bank pays you for keeping your money in your account. It is calculated based on your balance and the time that you keep it in your account. For a savings account, the interest rate is 3.5% per year."

Little David nodded and said, "I think I understand. Thank you for explaining everything to me."

Miss Smith smiled and said, "You're welcome, Little David. You are such a smart boy! You are such a good listener! Thank you for being interested in opening a bank account with us!"

She said, "Are you ready to open your account now?"

Little David looked at his dad and said, "Yes, I am."

His dad nodded and said, "Yes, we are."

Miss Smith said, "Great! Let's do it then!"

She took out some forms and a pen and gave them to them. She said, "These are the forms that you need to fill out and sign to open your account. They have some information and some terms and conditions that you need to agree to. Do you need any help with them?"

His dad said, "No, thank you. We can do it ourselves."

He helped Little David fill out and sign the forms. They wrote their names and addresses and phone numbers and email addresses. They chose a PIN number for Little David's ATM card. They agreed to the terms and conditions of the savings account.

They gave the forms and the pen back to Miss Smith. She checked them and said, "Everything looks good. Thank you for filling out the forms."

She took out an envelope and a card and gave them to Little David. She said, "This is your ATM card and this is your envelope. Your ATM card has your name and your account number on it. Your envelope has your PIN number inside it. Don't lose them or share them with anyone else."

She took out a receipt and a sticker and gave them to Little David. She said, "This is your receipt and this is your sticker. Your receipt shows how much money you deposited into your account today. Your sticker has your online banking username and password on it. You can use them to access your account online."

She took out a booklet and a keychain and gave them to Little David. She said, "This is your booklet and this is your keychain. Your booklet has some information and tips on how to use your account and how to save money. Your keychain has our logo and our phone number on it. You can use it to keep your keys or to call us if you have any questions or problems."

She smiled and said, "Congratulations, Little David! You have successfully opened your bank account with us! You are now a valued customer of our bank! We hope you enjoy your account and your gifts!"

She shook his hand and said, "Thank you for choosing our bank today!"

Little David shook her hand and said, "Thank you for helping me open my account today!"

He looked at his dad and said, "Dad, thank you for taking me to the bank today!"

His dad hugged him and said, "You're welcome, Little David! You are such a big boy! You are such a good saver!

He said, "You made me very happy today, David! I'm so proud of you!"

Little David felt happy too. He said, "You're welcome, dad! I'm glad I could make you happy! I love you!"

They hugged each other again and thanked Miss Smith again. They left the bank and got in the car. They drove back to their house.

Little David learned that opening a bank account can be easy and fun. He decided to use his account wisely and save his money for the future.

CHAPTER XIV
Little David Gets a Debit Card

One day, he decided to get a debit card with his mom. He asked his mom if he could go with her to the bank and she said yes. She gave him some money that he had earned from doing chores and told him to put it in his wallet. She also told him to bring his ID card and his bank account number.

Little David packed his wallet with his money and his cards. He put on his jacket and his shoes and went outside. He got in the car with his mom and drove to the bank. He thought, "I wonder what it's like to have a debit card. Maybe I can buy things without using cash or checks."

He got to the bank and saw a big sign that said "Welcome to the Bank". He felt excited and entered the bank.

He saw a lot of people and machines in the bank. He saw people who were wearing suits and ties and name tags. They were called bankers or tellers or managers. He followed his mom to a counter where a friendly man was sitting. He had a name tag that said "Mr. Brown".

He smiled and said, "Hello, how can I help you today?"

His mom said, "Hello, Mr. Brown. We would like to get a debit card for my son, Little David."

Mr. Brown said, "Sure, we can do that. Do you have your ID cards and your bank account number with you?"

His mom said, "Yes, we do." She took out her wallet and gave Mr. Brown her ID card and her bank account number. She also took out

Little David's wallet and gave Mr. Brown his ID card and his bank account number.

Mr. Brown scanned their cards and typed something on his computer. He said, "Okay, I have your information here. What kind of debit card would you like to get for Little David?"

His mom said, "We would like to get a basic debit card for him. He wants to spend his money at stores or online."

Mr. Brown said, "That's a good choice. A basic debit card is a card that lets you pay for things directly from your bank account. You don't need to use cash or checks or credit cards. You just need to swipe your card or enter your PIN number and follow the instructions on the screen."

He took out a brochure and showed it to them. It had pictures and words that explained the features and benefits of a basic debit card. It said things like "No annual fees", "Free ATM withdrawals", "Free online banking", "Free fraud protection", "Spending limit of $500 per day", and more.

He said, "These are some of the things that you get when you get a basic debit card with us. Do you have any questions?"

Little David looked at the brochure and asked, "What is an annual fee?"

Mr. Brown said, "An annual fee is a fee that some banks charge you for having a debit card with them. They deduct it from your balance every year. But we don't charge you any annual fees for having a basic debit card with us."

Little David asked, "What is an ATM withdrawal?"

Mr. Brown said, "An ATM withdrawal is when you take out money from your account at an ATM machine. You can use your debit card to do that. You can also use it to check your balance or transfer money or change your PIN number."

Little David asked, "What is online banking?"

Mr. Brown said, "Online banking is a service that lets you access your account from your computer or your phone or your tablet. You can check your balance, transfer money, pay bills, and more."

Little David asked, "What is fraud protection?"

Mr. Brown said, "Fraud protection is a service that protects your account from unauthorized or fraudulent transactions. If someone tries to use your card without your permission or knowledge, we will alert you and block the transaction. We will also refund you any money that you lose due to fraud."

Little David asked, "What is a spending limit?"

Mr. Brown said, "A spending limit is the maximum amount of money that you can spend with your card in a day. It helps you control your spending and avoid overdrafts or fees. For a basic debit card, the spending limit is $500 per day." Little David nodded and said, "I think I understand. Thank you for explaining everything to me."

Mr. Brown smiled and said, "You're welcome, Little David. You are such a smart boy! Thank you for being interested in getting a debit card with us!"

He said, "Are you ready to get your card now?"

Little David looked at his mom and said, "Yes, I am."

His mom nodded and said, "Yes, we are."

Mr. Brown said, "Great! Let's do it then!"

He took out a machine and a card and gave them to Little David. He said, "This is your debit card and this is the machine. Your debit card has your name and your account number on it. The machine will activate your card and let you choose your PIN number."

He showed Little David how to use the machine and the card. He said, "You need to insert your card into the machine and follow the instructions on the screen. You need to enter your date of birth and then choose a four-digit PIN number that only you know. You need to enter it twice to confirm it. Then you need to take out your card and keep it safe."

Little David followed Mr. Brown's instructions and used the machine and the card. He inserted his card into the machine and entered his date of birth. He chose a PIN number that he could remember and entered it twice. He took out his card and put it in his wallet.

The machine beeped and printed out a receipt that said "Your debit card has been activated". It also had some information and tips on how to use his card safely and securely.

Mr. Brown took the receipt and gave it to Little David. He said, "Congratulations, Little David! You have successfully got your debit card with us! You are now ready to use your card at any store or online! We hope you enjoy your card and your purchases!"

He shook his hand and said, "Thank you for choosing our bank today!"

Little David shook his hand and said, "Thank you for helping me get my card today!"

He looked at his mom and said, "Mom, thank you for taking me to the bank today!"

His mom hugged him as well.

CHAPTER XV
Little David Shops Online

Little David decided to shop online with his mom. He asked his mom if he could use her laptop and she said yes. She gave him her laptop and told him to be careful and not to buy anything without her permission. She also told him to use a website that she had bookmarked for him. Little David opened the laptop and went to the website that his mom had bookmarked. It was a website that had a lot of things for sale online. It had categories like "Books", "Toys", "Games", "Clothes", and more. It also had ratings and reviews from other customers. He thought, "Wow! There are so many things to buy here! I wonder if they have the video game that I want."

He decided to look for the video game that he wanted. He clicked on the category that said "Games" and saw a lot of games for different consoles and devices. He saw games like "Super Mario", "Minecraft", "Fortnite", and more. He thought, "These games look fun! But I want the game that my friend has." He typed the name of the game that he wanted in the search box. It was a game that his friend had shown him at school. It was a game that had cars and races and stunts and challenges. It was called "Need for Speed".

He pressed enter and saw a lot of results for the game. He saw different versions and editions and prices and sellers. He thought, "How do I choose the best one? Maybe I can read the ratings and reviews."

He clicked on one of the results that had a high rating and a low price. He saw a picture of the game and some details about it. It said things like "Need for Speed: Heat", "PS4", "New", "$19.99", "Free Shipping", and more.

He scrolled down and saw some ratings and reviews from other customers who had bought the game. They had stars and comments that said things like "Great game!", "Fast delivery!", "Awesome graphics!", and more.

He thought, "This game looks good! And it's cheap! And it has free shipping! I want to buy it!"

He looked at his mom and said, "Mom, can I buy this game? It's only $19.99 and it has free shipping!"

His mom looked at the laptop and saw the game that he wanted. She said, "Let me see it."

She took the laptop from him and checked the game and the seller. She said, "This game looks okay. And the seller has good ratings and reviews. And the price is reasonable. And it has free shipping. Okay, you can buy it."

She gave him back the laptop and said, "But you have to use your own money from your bank account. And you have to be careful with your debit card information. And you have to track your order and wait for it to arrive."

Little David nodded and said, "Okay, mom. Thank you for letting me buy it."

He clicked on the button that said "Add to Cart". He saw a pop-up window that said "Your item has been added to your cart". He clicked on another button that said "Proceed to Checkout".

He saw a page that asked him to enter his shipping address and his payment method. He entered his name and address and phone number in the fields provided. He chose his debit card as his payment method and entered his card number and expiration date and security code in the fields provided.

He checked his order summary and saw that everything was correct. He saw that his total amount was $19.99, that he had enough money in his bank account to cover it. He clicked on another button that said "Place Your Order".

He saw a confirmation page that said "Thank you for your order". It also had an order number and a tracking number and an estimated delivery date. It said that he would receive an email with more details about his order.

He thought, "Yay! I did it! I bought the game online! I can't wait to play it!"

He looked at his mom and said, "Mom, I bought the game! It was easy and fast and safe!"

His mom looked at the laptop and saw the confirmation page. She said, "Good job, Little David! You bought the game online! You are such a big boy! Thank you for being careful with your money and your card!"

She said, I'm so proud of you!"

Little David felt happy. He said, "You're welcome, mom! I love you!"

They hugged each other and closed the laptop. They went to have lunch with his dad and his baby sister.

Little David learned that shopping online can be easy and fun.

CHAPTER XVI
Little David Learns About Scams

On that day, David decided to learn about scams that people do online. He asked his mom if he could use her laptop and she said yes. She gave him her laptop and told him to be careful and not to click on anything suspicious. She also told him to use a website that she had bookmarked for him.

Little David opened the laptop and went to the website that his mom had bookmarked. It was a website that had information and pictures of different scams from around the world. It had categories like "Online shopping and auction scams", "Money mule scams", "Lottery and prize-winning scams", "Tax scams", and more. It also had tips on how to avoid them. He thought, "Wow! There are so many scams online! I wonder what they look like and how they work."

He decided to start with the category that said "Online shopping and auction scams". He clicked on it and saw a lot of examples of scams that people do when they sell or buy things online. He saw things like "Fake websites", "Fake products", "Fake reviews", "Fake payments", and more. He thought, "These scams look real! But they are not! They are ways of tricking people into giving money or personal details for nothing!"

He clicked on one of the examples that said "Fake websites". He saw a picture of a website that looked like a real online store. It had a logo and a name and a slogan that said "The best deals online". It had pictures and prices of products that looked attractive and cheap. It had buttons and links that said things like "Buy now", "Add to cart", "Checkout", and more.

He scrolled down and saw some tips on how to spot a fake website. They said things like:

- Check the URL of the website. Fake websites may have misspelled words or extra characters or numbers in their web address.
- Check the security of the website. Fake websites may not have a padlock icon or an HTTPS prefix in their web address, which means they are not secure or encrypted.
- Check the contact details of the website. Fake websites may not have a phone number or an email address or a physical address, or they may have fake ones that don't work or don't match their location.
- Check the reviews of the website. Fake websites may have no reviews or only positive reviews or reviews that are copied from other sources.

He thought, "These tips are useful! I can use them to check if a website is real or fake!"

He decided to try it out. He typed the URL of the website that he saw in the picture in his browser. He checked the URL and saw that it had a misspelled word and an extra number in it. He checked the security and saw that it didn't have a padlock icon or an HTTPS prefix in it. He checked the contact details and saw that it didn't have a phone number or an email address or a physical address. He checked the reviews and saw that it had no reviews at all.

He thought, "This website is fake! It is a scam! I'm glad I didn't click on anything!"

He closed the tab and went back to the website that his mom had bookmarked. He clicked on another category that said "Money mule scams". He saw a lot of examples of scams that people do when they ask others to move money for them online. He saw things like "Job offers", "Romance requests", "Charity appeals", "Lottery winnings", and more. He thought, "These scams look nice! But they are not! They are ways of using people to move money from illegal activities without being traced!"

CHAPTER XVII
Little David Sets a Goal

This time, Little David decided to set a goal for himself. He asked his mom if she could help him with it and she said yes. She gave him a notebook and a pen and told him to write down his goal and how he would reach it. She also told him to use a website that she had bookmarked for him.

Little David opened the notebook and wrote down his goal. He thought about what he really wanted to do or have or be. He thought about what would make him happy and proud and fulfilled. He thought about what would challenge him and help him grow and learn.

He decided that his goal was to learn how to play the guitar. He had always loved music and wanted to make his own songs. He had seen his uncle play the guitar at family gatherings and thought it was cool and fun. He wanted to be like him.

He wrote down his goal in his notebook. He made sure that his goal was clear and measurable and realistic. He wrote:

My goal is to learn how to play the guitar by the end of this year.

He looked at his mom and said, "Mom, this is my goal. Do you think I can do it?"

His mom looked at his notebook and said, "That's a great goal, Little David! I think you can do it if you work hard and have fun!"

She gave him a hug and said, "But you need to have a plan for how you will reach your goal. You need to break down your goal into smaller steps and actions that you can do every day or every week."

She opened the laptop and went to the website that she had bookmarked. It was a website that had information and pictures of how to set goals for kids. It had categories like "Identify the Goal", "Talk about the Purpose of the Goal", "Establish a Time Frame", "Make a Game Plan Using a Template or Worksheet", and "Track Progress, Provide Support, and Celebrate".

She said, "This website will help you make a plan for your goal. It will show you how to set effective goals and achieve them."

She clicked on the category that said "Talk about the Purpose of the Goal". She saw some tips on how to explain why the goal was important and meaningful. They said things like:

- Think about how your goal will benefit you or others.
- Think about how your goal will make you feel or what you will learn.
- Think about how your goal will align with your values or interests.

She said, "Let's talk about why you want to learn how to play the guitar. What are some of the benefits or feelings or values that you associate with your goal?"

Little David thought about it and said, "I want to learn how to play the guitar because:

- It will make me happy and creative.
- It will help me express myself and share my music with others.
- It will challenge me and teach me new skills.
- It will connect me with my uncle and other musicians."

He wrote down these reasons in his notebook under his goal. He said, "These are some of the reasons why I want to learn how to play the guitar."

His mom smiled and said, "Those are good reasons, Little David! You have a clear purpose for your goal. That will motivate you and keep you focused."

She clicked on the category that said "Establish a Time Frame". She saw some tips on how to set a deadline for the goal and break it down into smaller time periods. They said things like:

- Choose a realistic and specific date for when you want to achieve your goal.
- Divide your goal into smaller sub goals that you can achieve in shorter time periods, such as months, weeks, or days.
- Set milestones or checkpoints to track your progress and celebrate your achievements along the way.

She said, "Let's set a time frame for your goal. When do you want to learn how to play the guitar by?"

Little David thought about it and said, "I want to learn how to play the guitar by the end of this year. That's about 10 months from now."

He wrote down his deadline in his notebook under his goal. He said, "This is when I want to learn how to play the guitar by."

His mom nodded and said, "That's a good deadline, Little David! You have enough time to learn how to play the guitar, but not too much time that you lose interest or forget about your goal."

She said, "But you need to break down your goal into smaller sub goals that you can achieve in shorter time periods. What are some of the things that you need to do or learn to play the guitar?"

Little David thought about it and said, "I need to:

- Get a guitar and some accessories, like a tuner and a pick.
- Learn how to hold and tune the guitar.
- Learn how to read guitar tabs and chords.
- Learn how to play some basic songs and practice them regularly.

- Learn how to play some advanced songs and techniques."

He wrote down these sub goals in his notebook under his goal. He said, "These are some of the things that I need to do or learn to play the guitar."

His mom said, "Those are good sub goals, Little David! You have a clear plan for what you need to do or learn to play the guitar. That will help you stay organized and focused."

She said, "But you need to set milestones or checkpoints for each sub goal. How will you know if you have achieved each sub goal? How will you measure your progress and celebrate your achievements?"

Little David thought about it and he said, "That's a good idea Mom" and he set the milestones and the checkpoints for each sub goal as well.

CHAPTER XVIII
Little David Starts a Business

Little David decided that he wanted to open his own business and sell his creations to other people. He thought that would be a great way to earn some money and share his talents with the world. He also wanted to learn more about how businesses work and what it takes to be successful.

But how could he start his own business? He didn't know much about it and he didn't have a lot of resources. He decided to ask his parents, his teacher for some advice. They were very supportive of his idea and gave him some tips on how to plan and achieve his goal.

They told him that the first step was to do some research and find out what kind of products people would like to buy and how much they would pay for them. They suggested that he could look online, visit some local shops, or talk to his potential customers.

The second step was to make a budget and figure out how much it would cost him to make his products and how much profit he could make from selling them. They explained that he would need to consider the cost of materials, tools, packaging, transportation, and marketing. The third step was to create a brand name and a logo for his business and design some attractive labels and flyers to promote his products. They advised him that he should choose a name that reflects his personality and style and a logo that catches people's attention and makes them curious.

The fourth step was to find a place where he could sell his products and set up his shop. They recommended that he could start small and sell at local fairs, markets, or events where he could reach a lot of customers. They also suggested that he could create a website or a social media page where he could showcase his products online and take orders from anywhere. The fifth step was to keep track of his sales and expenses and evaluate his progress. They taught him how to use a spreadsheet or an app to record his income and costs and calculate his profit or loss. They also encouraged him to ask for feedback from his customers and improve his products based on their suggestions.

Little David followed their advice and worked hard on his business plan. He did his research and found out that people liked colorful and unique items that they could use or display in their homes or offices. He decided to make some paintings, sculptures, magnets, bookmarks, coasters, and keychains with different themes and designs.

He made a budget and found out that he could buy most of the materials from a local craft store at a reasonable price. He also used some recycled or donated items that he found at home or from his friends. He calculated that he could sell each item for $5-$10 depending on the size and complexity and make a profit of $2-$7 per item.

He created a brand name and a logo for his business and called it "David's Dazzling Designs". He chose a bright yellow color for his logo and wrote his name in a fun font with stars around it. He printed some labels and flyers with his logo and contact information and attached them to his products and distributed them around his neighborhood.

He found a place where he could sell his products and registered for a local craft fair that was happening next weekend. He borrowed a table and a tent from his parents and set up his shop at the fair. He displayed his products neatly on the table with signs showing the prices. He also brought some business cards with his website address where people could see more of his work online.

He kept track of his sales and expenses using an app on his phone. He sold 20 items on the first day of the fair and made $120 in revenue. He spent $40 on materials, $10 on transportation, $10 on registration fee, $5 on printing, $5 on snacks, $5 on tips, $5 on taxes, totaling $80 in expenses. He made $40 in profit on the first day.

He asked for feedback from his customers and learned what they liked or disliked about his products. He found out that they liked the variety of themes and designs, the quality of materials, the creativity of shapes, the durability of finishes, the usefulness of functions, the affordability of prices, the attractiveness of packaging, the friendliness of service, the professionalism of presentation, and the convenience of online ordering.

He improved his products based on their suggestions. He added more themes such as animals, sports, music, nature, etc. He used more colors such as blue, green, purple,

He experimented with different materials such as clay, wood, metal, etc. He made different shapes such as circles, squares, triangles, etc. He applied different finishes such as glossy, matte, glittery, etc. He added more functions such as magnets, clips, hooks, etc. He lowered some prices and raised some others depending on the demand and supply. He made some special offers such as buy one get one free, free shipping, etc. He improved his packaging with some ribbons, stickers, tags, etc. He smiled more and thanked his customers for their support.

He sold 30 items on the second day of the fair and made $180 in revenue. He spent $60 on materials, $10 on transportation, $10 on registration fee, $5 on printing, $5 on snacks, $5 on tips, $5 on taxes, totaling $100 in expenses. He made $80 in profit on the second day.

He was very happy with his results and proud of his achievements. He learned a lot about running a business and had a lot of fun doing it. He decided to continue his business and expand it to other venues and platforms. He also decided to donate some of his profits to a local charity that helped children in need.

He thanked his parents and his teacher for their advice and guidance and gave them some of his products as gifts. They were very proud of him and congratulated him on his success. They told him that he had a bright future ahead of him and that they would always support him in his dreams.

Little David was a thirsty and adventurous boy who loved to drink lemonade. He enjoyed making his own lemonade with fresh lemons, sugar, water, and ice. He had a lot of fun experimenting with different flavors and colors by adding some fruits, herbs, or syrups.

One day, he decided that he wanted to open his own business and sell his lemonade to other people. He thought that would be a great way to quench his thirst and make some friends. He also wanted to learn more about how lemonade works and what it takes to be delicious.

But how could he start his own business? He didn't know much about it and he didn't have a lot of equipment. He decided to ask his grandma for some help. She was very supportive of his idea and gave him some tips on how to plan and achieve his goal.

She told him that the first step was to choose a recipe and make a batch of lemonade. She suggested that he could use her old cookbook, look online, or create his own recipe. She also gave him some lemons from her garden and some sugar from her pantry.

The second step was to taste and test his lemonade and make sure it was good. She explained that he would need to consider the sweetness, sourness, freshness, and temperature of his lemonade. She also gave him some cups and spoons to try his lemonade.

The third step was to name and decorate his lemonade and make it stand out from the crowd. She advised him that he should choose a name that reflects his personality and taste and a decoration that catches people's eyes and makes them thirsty.

The fourth step was to find a location where he could sell his lemonade and set up his stand. She recommended that he could start small and sell at his front yard, sidewalk, or park where he could reach a lot of customers. She also gave him some cardboard, markers, and scissors to make a sign for his stand.

The fifth step was to keep track of his sales and expenses and evaluate his progress. She taught him how to use a notebook or an app to record his income and costs and calculate his profit or loss. She also encouraged him to ask for feedback from his customers and improve his lemonade based on their suggestions.

Little David followed his grandma's advice and worked hard on his business plan. He chose a recipe and made a batch of lemonade. He used four lemons, half a cup of sugar, four cups of water, and some ice cubes. He also added some strawberries and mint leaves for extra flavor and color.

He tasted and tested his lemonade and made sure it was good. He found out that it was sweet, sour, fresh, and cold enough for his liking. He also asked his grandma and some friends to try his lemonade and they all liked it too.

He named and decorated his lemonade and made it stand out from the crowd. He called it "David's Super Strawberry Mint Lemonade". He chose a bright pink color for his lemonade and wrote his name in a cool font with stars around it. He also added some straws, napkins, and stickers to his lemonade.

He found a location where he could sell his lemonade and set up his stand. He decided to sell at the park where there were a lot of people playing and having fun. He borrowed a table and a cooler from his grandma and set up his stand at the park. He displayed his lemonade neatly on the table with a sign showing the price. He also brought some change and a tip jar with him.

He kept track of his sales and expenses using a notebook on his phone. He sold 25 cups of lemonade on the first day and made $25 in revenue. He spent $5 on lemons, $1 on sugar, $1 on water, $1 on ice, $2 on strawberries, $1 on mint leaves, $2 on cups, $1 on spoons, $1 on straws, $1 on napkins, $1 on stickers, totaling $16 in expenses. He made $9 in profit on the first day.

He asked for feedback from his customers and learned what they liked or disliked about his lemonade. He found out that they liked the taste, smell, color, and temperature of his lemonade. They also liked the name, decoration, and service of his lemonade. They said that his lemonade was super delicious and refreshing.

He improved his lemonade based on their suggestions. He added more strawberries and mint leaves to make it more flavorful and colorful. He also added some honey and lemon zest to make it more sweet and sour. He lowered the price to $0.75 per cup to attract more customers. He also made some special offers such as buy two get one free, free refill, etc. He improved his sign with some glitter and stickers to make it more eye-catching.

He sold 40 cups of lemonade on the second day and made $30 in revenue. He spent $8 on lemons, $2 on sugar, $2 on water, $2 on ice, $4 on strawberries, $2 on mint leaves, $3 on honey, $1 on lemon zest, $3 on cups, $1 on spoons, $1 on straws, $1 on napkins, $1 on stickers, totaling $31 in expenses. He made -$1 in profit on the second day.

He was not very happy with his results but he was not discouraged either, he learned from his mistakes. He learned a lot about running a business and had a lot of fun doing it. He decided to continue his business and adjust it to make it more profitable. He introduced "DIY" Lemonade. He set up a table with different flavors of lemonade and a variety of toppings, like sliced fruit and candy. He even provided instructions on how to mix and match the flavors to create your own unique drink. Kids and adults alike were intrigued by Little David's unique lemonade stand and the challenge of creating their own tasty concoctions. He also created PREMIUM LEMONADE with a premium price, which was using FRESH Organic ingredient and shake them as normally we do for Cocktail! Before he knew it, he was making more money than he ever had before!

He also decided to save some of his money for a new blender that he wanted to buy. He thanked his grandma for her help and support and gave her some of his lemonade as a gift. She was very proud of him and congratulated him on his effort. She told him that he had a lot of potential and that she would always help him in his dreams.

From his grandma, his parents and his teachers, Little David learned a lot of things, such as:

Fixed asset: This is the asset that is not consumed or sold during the normal course of business, such as a table, a cooler, a blender, etc. For this lemonade business, let's assume that Little David borrows a table and a cooler from his grandma and buys a blender for $50. So his fixed asset is $50.

Current asset: This is the asset that is consumed or sold during the normal course of business, such as cash, inventory, etc. For this lemonade business, let's assume that Little David has $100 in cash to start with and buys some inventory such as lemons, sugar, water, ice, cups, spoons, straws, napkins, stickers, etc. Let's say he spends $16 on inventory for the first day and $31 for the second day. So his current asset is $100 - $16 - $31 – $53.

Material: This is the cost of the raw materials used to make the product, such as lemons, sugar, water, ice, etc. For this lemonade business, let's assume that Little David uses four lemons ($1), half a cup of sugar ($0.25), four cups of water ($0.25), and some ice cubes ($0.25) to make one batch of lemonade. He also adds some strawberries ($1) and mint leaves ($0.5) for extra flavor and color. So his material cost per batch is $3.25.

Labor: This is the cost of the human effort involved in making the product or providing the service, such as wages, salaries, tips, etc. For this lemonade business, let's assume that Little David does all the work by himself and does not pay himself any wages or salaries. However, he does receive some tips from his customers. Let's say he gets $5 in tips on the first day and $10 on the second day. So his labor income is $5 + $10 = $15.

Gross profit: This is the difference between the revenue (the money earned from selling the product or service) and the cost of goods sold (the total cost of making or buying the product or service), excluding other expenses such as taxes, fees, etc. For this lemonade business, let's assume that Little David sells 25 cups of lemonade at $1 per cup on the first day and 40 cups of lemonade at $0.75 per cup on the second day. So his revenue is 25 x $1 + 40 x $0.75 = $55. His cost of goods sold is the material cost per batch multiplied by the number of batches he makes. Let's say he makes one batch on the first day and two batches on the second day. So his cost of goods sold is $3.25 x 1 + $3.25 x 2 = $9.75. So his gross profit is $55 - $9.75 = $45.25.

Net profit after tax: This is the difference between the gross profit and all other expenses such as taxes, fees, transportation, printing, etc. For this lemonade business, let's assume that Little David pays $5 in taxes and $10 in fees for the registration and the permit to sell at the park. He also spends $10 on transportation to and from the park and $5 on printing his signs and flyers. So his total expenses are $5 + $10 + $10 + $5 = $30. So his net profit after tax is $45.25 - $30 = $15.25.

So to summarize, Little David's lemonade business has a fixed asset of $50, a current asset of $53, a material cost of $3.25 per batch, a labor income of $15, a gross profit of $45.25, and a net profit after tax of $15.25.

To answer your other questions, Little David can sell 65 cups of lemonade in two days, which is about 975 cups per month if he sells every day. Little David knew, that this was an estimation only, because the demand for lemonade may vary depending on the weather, the season, the location, the competition, etc. So Little David knew that he may need to adjust his business plan accordingly.

Little David understood about how much money was required for his lemonade business and how to calculate the profit and loss.

CHAPTER XIX
Little David Achieves His Dream

We knew that Little David was a hard-working and ambitious boy who loved to run his lemonade business. He enjoyed making and selling his delicious lemonade to his customers and earning some money from his sales. He had a lot of fun experimenting with new recipes and strategies to grow his business.

One day, he decided that he wanted to achieve his dream of becoming financially independent from his lemonade business. He thought that would be a great way to secure his future and pursue his passions. He also wanted to learn more about how money works and what it takes to be wealthy.

But how could he achieve his dream of financial independence? He didn't know much about it and he didn't have a lot of resources. He decided to ask his uncle for some help. He was very supportive of his idea and gave him some tips on how to plan and achieve his goal.

He told him that the first step was to set a specific and realistic goal for his financial independence. He suggested that he could use the 4% rule, which states that you can withdraw 4% of your savings every year without running out of money. He also gave him a calculator to help him figure out how much money he would need to save.

The second step was to track his income and expenses and create a budget for his lemonade business. He explained that he would need to know how much money he was making and spending every month and how much profit he was keeping. He also gave him a spreadsheet or an app to help him record his numbers.

The third step was to save and invest his money wisely and grow his wealth over time. He advised him that he should save at least 10% of his income every month and invest it in a diversified portfolio of stocks, bonds, real estate, etc. He also gave him some books and podcasts to help him learn more about investing.

The fourth step was to increase his income and reduce his expenses and boost his savings rate. He recommended that he could find new ways to attract more customers and sell more lemonade, such as offering discounts, referrals, loyalty programs, etc. He also suggested that he could cut down on unnecessary costs, such as buying in bulk, using coupons, recycling, etc.

The fifth step was to monitor his progress and adjust his plan as needed. He taught him how to use a chart or a graph to visualize his savings growth and compare it with his goal. He also encouraged him to celebrate his milestones and reward himself for his achievements.

Little David followed his uncle's advice and worked hard on his financial plan. He set a specific and realistic goal for his financial independence. He decided that he wanted to have $1 million in savings by the time he was 25 years old. He used the 4% rule and calculated that he would need to save $40,000 per year or $3,333 per month or $111 per day.

He tracked his income and expenses and created a budget for his lemonade business. He found out that he was making $2,000 per month in revenue from selling 80 cups of lemonade per day at $0.75 per cup. He also found out that he was spending $1,000 per month in expenses for buying lemons, sugar, water, ice, cups, spoons, straws, napkins, stickers, taxes, fees, transportation, printing, etc. So his profit was $1,000 per month or $33 per day.

He saved and invested his money wisely and grew his wealth over time. He saved 10% of his income every month and invested it in a diversified portfolio of stocks, bonds, real estate, etc. He earned an average return of 8% per year on his investments. He also reinvested his dividends and interest to take advantage of compound interest.

He increased his income and reduced his expenses and boosted his savings rate. He found new ways to attract more customers and sell more lemonade, such as offering discounts, referrals, loyalty programs, etc. He also cut down on unnecessary costs, such as buying in bulk, using coupons, recycling, etc. He increased his revenue to $3,000 per month and decreased his expenses to $500 per month. So his profit was $2,500 per month or $83 per day.

He monitored his progress and adjusted his plan as needed. He used a chart or a graph to visualize his savings growth and compare it with his goal. He also celebrated his milestones and rewarded himself for his achievements. He bought himself a new bike when he reached $10,000 in savings. He took a trip to Disneyland when he reached $100,000 in savings. He donated some of his money to a charity when he reached $500,000 in savings.

He achieved his dream of financial independence from his lemonade business. He reached $1 million in savings by the time he was 25 years old. He used the 4% rule and withdrew $40,000 per year or $3,333 per month or $111 per day from his savings without running out of money. He was free to pursue his passions and live his life on his own terms.

He thanked his uncle for his help and support and gave him some of his lemonade as a gift. He was very proud of him and congratulated him on his success. He told him that he had a bright future ahead of him and that he would always help him in his dreams.

Don't miss out!

Visit the website below and you can sign up to receive emails whenever The Blessed Creation publishes a new book. There's no charge and no obligation.

https://books2read.com/r/B-A-XGAX-DCOHC

BOOKS 2 READ

Connecting independent readers to independent writers.

Also by The Blessed Creation

How to Pray a Good Prayer and Simple Guide for Normal People and
Get Answered (With Testimonies)
Panda Panda Bear What Do You Learn: With Jokes and Quizzes
Little David Learns to Earn a Lot of Money

About the Author

ABOUT THE AUTHOR

The Blessed Creation is The Home of one Family with several persons. All Family Members grew a passion to empower people to live life to the fullest. We believe that everyone has the opportunity to get the right support around them.

The Blessed Creation believe that we will empower people for BETTER LIFE by sharing stories through publishing the great and awesome books. It is a GIFT to the WORLD.

Everyone has biggest passion about writing and creation for everything which are very good to share to the World. One of us is a freelance editor, has a Graduate Certificate of Editing and Publishing. This person has biggest passion to get perfecting book manuscripts for publication. He is passionate about art, including how to make beautiful book to share.

We have several artist who thinking outside the square and giving us a lot of ideas for our potential Buyers to enjoy.

Want to contact us ? Just drop an email to: theblessedcreation17@gmail.com